BEST WALKS ON THE LOWER LAKELAND FEI
In the South-East

The 'Lion and Lamb' on Helm Crag looking towards Dunmail Raise

BEST WALKS ON THE LOWER LAKELAND FELLS

In the South-East

Bob Allen

MICHAEL JOSEPH
London

MICHAEL JOSEPH LTD

Published by the Penguin Group
27 Wrights Lane, London W8 5TZ
Viking Penguin Inc., 375 Hudson Street, New York, New York 10014, USA
Penguin Books Australia Ltd, Ringwood, Victoria, Australia
Penguin Books Canada Ltd, 10 Alcorn Avenue, Toronto, Ontario,
Canada M4V 3B2
Penguin Books (NZ) Ltd, 182–190 Wairau Road, Auckland 10, New Zealand

Penguin Books Ltd, Registered Offices: Harmondsworth, Middlesex, England

First published in Great Britain 1995

Copyright © Bob Allen 1990, 1995
The majority of this material appears in *On Lower Lakeland Fells*
first published May 1990

Typeset in 11/12pt Linotron Goudy Old Style by
Goodfellow and Egan Ltd. Cambridge
Made and printed in Singapore by
Kyodo Printing Co. (s) Pte Ltd.

ISBN 0 7181 3808 2

The moral right of the author has been asserted

Also by Bob Allen

ON HIGH LAKELAND FELLS
ON LOWER LAKELAND FELLS
ESCAPE TO THE DALES
ON FOOT IN SNOWDONIA
SHORT WALKS IN THE LAKE DISTRICT

CONTENTS

Introduction   6

1. Elter Water, Colwith and Little Langdale   9
2. Tom Heights and Black Fell   13
3. Loughrigg Fell   17
4. High Pike and Scandale   21
5. Grasmere and Rydal   25
6. Butter Crag and Allcock Tarn   29
7. Wansfell Pike and Troutbeck   33
8. Silver How   37
9. Helm Crag and the Easedale Ridge   41
10. Whitbarrow Scar   45
Index   48

Acknowledgements

My debt to the Ordnance Survey and their wonderful maps will be self-evident. I have pored over them, searched my memories with their help and tramped over the fells with them in my pocket to remind me of details long forgotten.

My old friend Rob Rose accompanied me on several exploratory walks, my wife Lin and son Jonathan on others (and didn't complain much), but on the whole I have spent most of the time on the fells on my own with my two dogs, Henry and Freddie. Everybody else decided that waiting around while I took photographs was just too boring, so they left me to get on with it alone.

INTRODUCTION

This is an illustrated collection of ten of the best shorter fellwalks in the south-eastern part of the Lake District. While I was completing my first Lakeland book, *On High Lakeland Fells*, I was aware that all the emphasis in that book was on the 'High' and that I was missing out some marvellous fells whose only difference was their comparative lack of height. So I started looking and surprised myself with the quality and quantity of excellent shorter walks that can be found. The average altitude of this collection is 1200ft/366m, average height gained is 1000ft/305m, average distance 5¼ miles/8.4 km and the average time a little under three hours. All are 'rounds', enabling an easy return to the starting-point. If your own favourite fell is not included, that may be because I've tried to avoid overlapping with walks in the 'High Fells' book referred to above. If it's not in there, then I apologise: I had to draw a line some-where.

The **Map:**   All except one of the walks (Whitbarrow Scar) can be found on the Ordnance Survey Outdoor Leisure map, sheet 7, South Eastern area. However, don't rely too slavishly on the map: footpaths which are clearly marked on the map sometimes may be hardly distinguishable on the ground.

Distances: These are not exact, simply approximations based on the map.

'Highest elevation reached' and **'height gained':** These are the actual heights in feet above sea level (converted to metres) from precise figures on the map if given. If not, the height is my best assessment.

The **'star rating':**   This is completely subjective. I have simply attempted to convey something of the overall quality of the walk. Fine mountain landscape and scenery and variety of interest are particularly important in this assessment. I know I have a definite preference for the wild places, the rough ground, the untracked rather than the smooth pathways and this will no doubt be sometimes apparent. I respond above all to fine landscape scenery. I go to the fells and mountains for exercise and recreation but I live for those moments when I just have to grab for my camera.

'General level of exertion required':   The more steeply you go uphill the more likely you are to get puffed; a short but steep climb can be a lot more exhausting than a long level stroll. I have simply attempted to give some indication of what to expect.

'Time for the round': My times are not based on any formula, just an assessment based on my experience. They do *not* include lengthy lunch-stops.

'Terrain': In the introductory specifications for each walk I have added a few comments about the nature of the ground underfoot, which I hope will be helpful. Generally these refer to conditions in spring, summer or autumn; winter can introduce a new dimension of unpredictability which is the delight of experienced fellwalkers but could cause problems for beginners.

Clothing and footwear: The biggest cause of all accidents on the fells is slipping on wet grass and so the importance of suitable footwear – preferably warm, well-fitting, waterproof, giving support to the ankles and with suitably ridged soles – cannot be over-emphasised. Nor can I stress too strongly that mild, balmy weather in the valley can be transformed at 1500ft into something more like the Arctic; it helps enormously to wear clothing which minimises dampness caused by sweating and modern synthetic fabrics now do this. Mixing man-made and natural fibres defeats the object: wearing a Goretex-type breathable waterproof on top of a cotton shirt and a woollen jersey is unlikely to keep you dry.

Place names: I hope and believe I have used the spellings used on the relevant OS map, but there are minor alterations from one edition of those maps to another, and from one scale to another, so it will depend which edition of the relevant map you are looking at. Also, the walking and climbing community use some names which you will not find on the OS map. Where relevant, I have mentioned these in the text but have used the OS names.

Grid references: It helps greatly in not getting lost if you start from the right place so I have provided a grid reference for the starting point of each walk. The National Grid Reference System is explained in the bottom right-hand corner of the Ordnance Survey map for anybody who isn't accustomed to using it. Correct use of a compass, including checking your bearing before you are overtaken by the mist, will minimise your mixing up your lefts with your rights and heading off down the wrong valley. By not heeding this advice myself in the Alps I once failed to climb the wrong route on the wrong mountain. Despite all your instincts to the contrary, the compass is almost never wrong and magnetic rocks are very rare indeed: it is just that you are not where you thought you were.

Access: Across much of the Lake District there is a generally accepted freedom to roam on high land above the cultivated land or intake walls. It is essential, however, that public footpaths or permissive rights of way are used to reach the higher land and I have tried to ensure that no one will get into trouble through following my directions.

1.   Elter Water, Colwith and Little Langdale

Best Map: OS 1:25,000 S.E. Sheet (Windermere and Kendal)

Distance: 5½ miles/8.8km

Highest elevation reached: 550ft/168m approx.

Height gained: 300ft/91m

Overall star rating: * * *

General level of exertion required: Fairly low

Time for the round: About 2½ hours

Terrain: Easy walking on good, though sometimes inevitably muddy, paths. No problems even when the mist is down to valley level.

This walk doesn't actually go up onto any fells, low or otherwise, but every fellwalker needs a few low-level walks for the off-day, the wet day, the family day. This is one of the best, with a splendid succession of little lakes, woods and waterfalls. Its description could however easily turn into a list of gates and stiles (the lower down you are, the more there are of them!) and you'd still get lost, so I will only mention the vital ones, because once you get going it is actually all very straightforward.

A footpath is signed to Skelwith Bridge from the car park in Elterwater village (on the other side of the road from the Britannia Inn). Grid ref. 327047. Follow this beside the Great Langdale Beck and then alongside the beautiful Elter Water, rambling through fine open parkland with mature trees until you reach a gate and enter a wood where the path goes along the road for a short way, and very close to the torrent of water at Skelwith Force, before passing between the buildings of Kirkstone (Slate) Galleries. The main A593 road to Coniston is reached here, so turn right (south) and cross the river by the road bridge and walk along the road for about a hundred paces towards Coniston before turning off right on the public footpath signed for Colwith Bridge. This path now climbs through a little wood (parallel with the main road), joins a farm track, continues beyond the farm (Park House) as a path again with views overlooking the Elter Water meadows you walked through a little while ago, past some incongruous permanently sited caravans and between the substantial buildings of Park Farm (where there is an intriguing 'alphabet stone' set in a wall on the left).

An arrow on another wall now points the way, keeping to the path and only crossing metalled drives, by-passing Low Park Farm, and leading across the slope of a field before descending through woods towards the River Brathay (flowing from Little Langdale Tarn) at Colwith Bridge and a stile onto the road

Elter Water and the Langdale Pikes

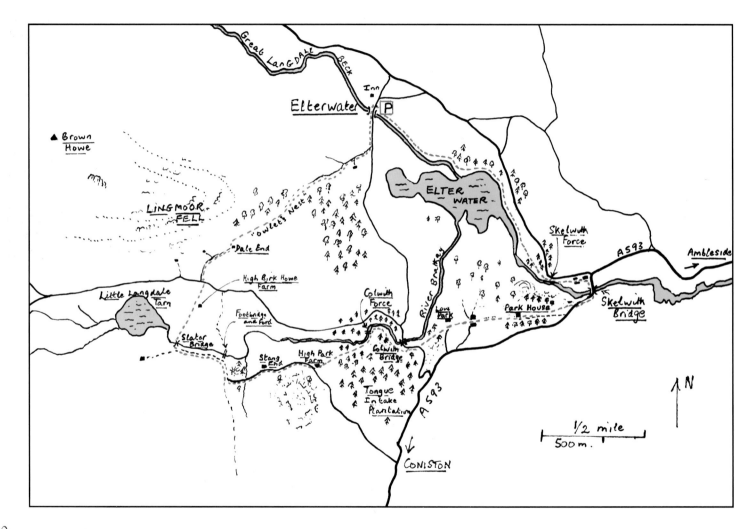

(Elterwater to Coniston). The fine waterfalls of Colwith Force are now close by upstream, so turn right along the road for fifty paces or so and climb another stile into the lovely woods (sign for Colwith Force). The better path meanders along above the river bank and soon the roar of the double cascade can first be heard and then seen, usually partly masked by foliage but a fine sight nonetheless. Attempts have obviously been made to harness the water-power as a little building at the foot of the torrent and to one side testifies.

Leaving the falls, the path continues through the woods on the left bank, climbing gently away from the stream and emerging by the buildings of High Park Farm. A bridleway passes between these and joins a metalled track just beyond them, giving, for the first time for some distance, the opportunity to see the line of the walk ahead as it crosses the valley bottom of Little Langdale and then contours right across the slopes of Lingmoor Fell. First, however, keep on the track as it winds round Stang End Farm and downhill over a cattle-grid, crosses a small beck, then curves round a tree-covered hillock to reveal a footbridge and a ford. If you cross here, you will miss one of the best bits of the walk so keep to the lane on the left bank which now has old quarry spoil on its left side. Beyond two gates, a stile in the wall on the right leads across to the gently pointed arch of the picturesque Slater Bridge. This spans the outflow from Little Langdale Tarn which can't be seen yet, though it soon comes into view, a lovely sheet of water backed

by the Tilberthwaite Fells. The way now leads up the fields towards Lingmoor Fell via High Birk Howe Farm.

Just beyond the farm, the track meets the road which runs through Little Langdale. Turn left and then immediately right and you are on the track, not marked on the map but known, I believe, as the 'Owlet's Nest' track. After passing Dale Head Farm, this soon becomes a rough lane, often between stone walls and beneath the trees, with a few surprise views to the Helvellyn massif. Keep to the right when there is a choice of ways and you are soon back once more on the road outside Elterwater and at the end of a delightful ramble.

Slater Bridge in Little Langdale

11

2.   Tom Heights and Black Fell

Best Map: OS 1:25,000 S.E. Sheet (Windermere
  and Kendal)

Distance: 5¾ miles/9.2km

Highest elevation reached: 1056ft/322m

Height gained: 932ft/284m

Overall star rating: */**

General level of exertion required: Low

Time for the round: 3–4 hours

Terrain: Generally good paths. Care needed with
  route-finding in high summer when visibility
  may be restricted by woods or bracken.

Black Fell rises above wooded slopes to the north-east of the attractive area of Tarn Hows, and Tom Heights is the high land just west of The Tarns. This walk is an attractive circuit linking all three.

Start from the car park by Glen Mary Bridge (grid ref. 322999) on the A593 between Ambleside and Coniston, just south of Yew Tree Tarn. Now take the good path to the east, signed for Tarn Hows, which rises up the left side of a very attractive wooded gill, passing a cascade and then a fine waterfall in a ravine, to reach a dam at the outflow from Tarn Hows. This whole area is beautifully maintained by the National Trust.

Turn left here on a good track which runs beside this most attractive small lake. About 300 yds beyond the dam, escape from the picnic parties by leaving the main track (at the point where the track itself goes away from the tarn) and turn left (north-west) on a path (not shown on the OS map) which climbs towards higher ground and is very obvious, except when possibly obscured by tall bracken. Open ground, with a sprinkling of silver birches, is soon reached as the path rises north to a broad ridge with several heathery and rocky tops. A cairned path links these to a heap of stones on the highest point, Tom Heights.

Coniston Water is now in sight, with Wetherlam, Crinkle Crags, Bowfell, Helvellyn and even High Street. So also, to the north-east across a depression, is Black Fell. A path undulates towards it, turning right downhill just before reaching a big cairn on a viewpoint. Keep left at the fork ahead and follow your nose down to pick up the main track again approaching a gate and ladder-stile on the bend of a walled lane. (This bend is at the head of a boggy

Black Fell seen from Tom Heights

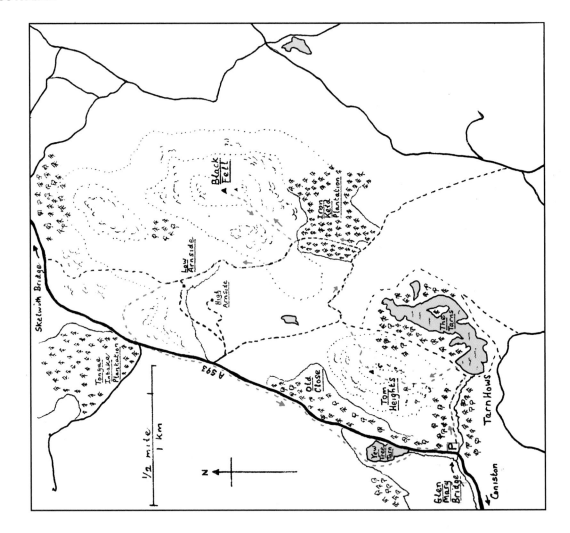

depression and a reedy tarn is visible at the northern end.)

Turn right, uphill, here along this rough lane and follow it round a bend, continuing to a public bridleway sign where you turn off left and into Iron Keld Plantation. Walking over drifted pine needles on a firm base, the path reaches a gate at the edge of the forest, and two stone gate posts immediately beyond. The bridlepath continues, but turn off it, sharp right, as soon as you are past the gate posts. A cairned path now climbs the fellside to the north-east, soon escaping the bracken and steering to a trig point on a little rocky summit.

A National Trust plaque fixed to it announces that this is Black Crag. The mountain scene featuring the Langdale Pikes to the north is good, as it is south-west to Wetherlam. The best views to Windermere are from a large circular cairn on a plinth about 200 yds south.

It is now best to retrace your steps to the bridle-path where it emerged from Iron Keld Plantation, then turn right and follow it generally north over pleasant grassland until it reaches attractive farm buildings at Low Arnside. Bear left (north-west) at the fork just beyond these (finger-post) and down a field to a gate in a wall-corner. It is then more steeply downhill, curving sharply left to reach the A593 opposite Tongue Intake Plantation.

Turn left here along the main road for 50 yds, then cross a ladder-stile and follow a series of footpaths parallel with the road, on its right, with traffic largely

out of sight. I could not locate the permissive path leading into woods just north of Old Close; it is shown on the OS map on the left-hand side of the road. Therefore I stayed on the path that continues on the right side until it curved away from the road and around the western margins of the lovely Yew Tree Tarn. Leaving this, the car park is only a few minutes further on.

View to the Langdale Pikes from near Low Arnside Farm

15

3. Loughrigg Fell

Best Map: OS 1:25,000 S.E. Sheet (Windermere and Kendal)

Distance: 4 miles/6.4km approx.

Highest elevation reached: 1099ft/335m

Height gained: 900ft/274m

Overall star rating: * */ * * *

General level of exertion required: Medium

Time for the round: 2½ hours

Terrain: The early part of this walk uses sheep tracks when they can be found, but then joins substantial and well-used paths for the descent and return.

Loughrigg Fell is justly popular with fellwalkers of all ages for, although of no great height, it is quite a complicated little mountain and gives some outstanding views in good visibility. Even in poor visibility, the main paths are clearly marked but still Loughrigg Fell has some secret places.

Probably the most popular ascent – because it's the most obvious – is the short way from the top of the Red Bank road between Grasmere and Langdale and on any fine weekend a stream of pilgrims will be seen toiling up it. A much better walk circles Loughrigg Tarn on its western side and then climbs steep slopes to the north-east to the triple summits. The drawback can be parking problems. My proposed route is not so obvious as either of the ways mentioned above; it climbs more gently over much less trodden (though occasionally boggy) ground and allows a return along Loughrigg Terrace with its wonderful views over Grasmere and Rydal Water.

The start is about a mile out of Ambleside on the A591, just before you reach Rydal where a bridge crosses the River Rothay. Turn sharp left here and then immediately right over a cattle-grid to find the car park a hundred yards further on the left (grid ref. 365059).

Leaving the car park, slant up the field as if towards Ambleside and go through a gate in the wall. A narrow path rounds the fell and climbs up beside the fine little crag of Lanty Scar (in summer this can be through bracken as well), working up a broad gully to gain more height. The path soon becomes less obvious but it is not hard going and the gully leads to a rocky high point, at the end of a long, curving and very broad ridge, from where there are fine views over Rydal Water to Nab Scar and the Fairfield Group of

Loughrigg Fell seen from the boat-landing on Grasmere

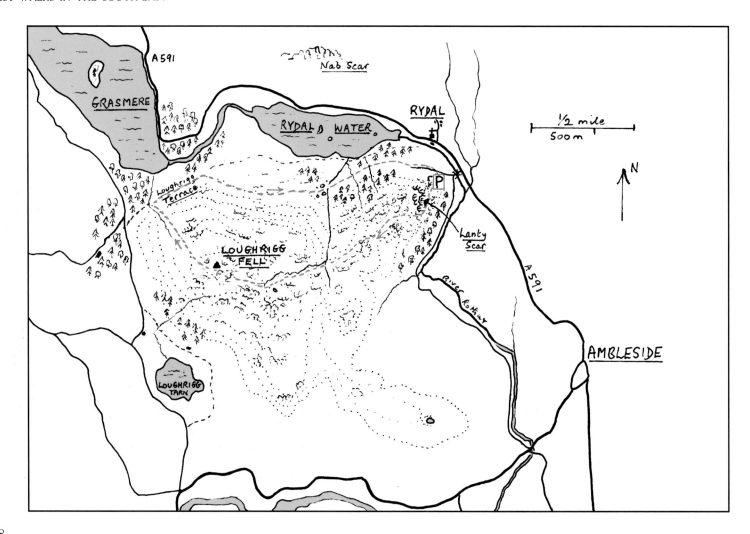

A 591

Nab Scar

GRASMERE

RYDAL WATER

RYDAL

½ mile
500m

Loughrigg Terrace

LOUGHRIGG FELL

Lanty Scar

N

River Rothay

A 591

AMBLESIDE

LOUGHRIGG TARN

fells. Further along is another rocky point and beyond that again is a substantial cairn. These landmarks all give the direction to take, following sheep tracks through the bracken before descending a little to cross the main grassy bridleway that links Rydal with Langdale.

Beyond a short boggy section is a maze of sheep tracks but choose those that lead generally up a long slope, between many small crags and scattered juniper bushes, in the general direction of the highest ground ahead. A little tarn is reached, not much bigger than a large puddle, and then a well-worn and much-cairned path. This leads up a couple of short slopes and the trig-point on the summit of Loughrigg Fell is reached. Once revived and the views admired, it is straightforward now and downhill all the way, following the path to the north-west in the general direction of Grasmere. The landscape seen on the descent is really outstanding; I never tire of that wonderful outlook over Rydal and Grasmere surrounded by such fine fells.

At the end of the steep section, turn right and join the excellent level path that runs along the Loughrigg Terrace. This leads gently to the prospect over Rydal Water and then, keeping on the higher level when the choice is presented, skirt below first one and then the second great cave on the way back towards Rydal. Don't descend to Rydal Water's edge but keep on the path on the higher level. This soon reaches a tarmac lane and the car park is just a short way along it.

Grasmere from Loughrigg Fell

19

4.   High Pike and Scandale

Best Map: OS 1:25,000 S.E. Sheet (Windermere
   and Kendal)

Distance: 8½ miles/13.6km approx.

Highest elevation reached: 2329ft/710m approx.

Height gained: 2181ft/665m

Overall star rating: * *

General level of exertion required: Medium

Time for the round: 4–4½ hours

Terrain: Almost all on good paths, with just a few
   boggy areas.

The west wall of the deep valley of Scandale, whose waters drain due south to Ambleside and Windermere, rises as a narrow and occasionally rocky ridge having two steps, Low Pike and High Pike. Their ascent gives an enjoyable walk, and the return down Scandale is easy and passes through some delightful landscape.

Start from Ambleside; the Rydal Road car park (grid ref. 376047) is probably the most convenient one to use. Cross the A591 from here and turn up the Kirkstone Road opposite, then up the first lane on the left, Nook Lane (to which some wag inevitably always adds a 'y'). The lane becomes a rough track and crosses Scandale Beck by Low Sweden Bridge at some falls in a well-wooded gill, then turns up the left bank. At the third gateway the now grassy track forks; continue ahead on the main branch which ambles along over grassy sheep pastures, with long views up quiet Scandale as far as Little Hart Crag's twin-topped summit on the skyline. After a gateway and sheepfold the path rises to some small rock buttresses (Sweden Crag and High and Low Brock Crags) colonised by trees. The path winds up through these to meet the ridge-top wall. Turn right alongside it and climb steadily towards the rocky peak of Low Pike, seen ahead. The path by-passes the top but it is worth visiting for a splendid view of the ridge rising ahead. This shortly becomes noticeably rockier but the wall, with the path beside it, continues resolutely along the crest as it rises to High Pike. There are one or two breaches, but it is a tribute to the skill of the wall-builders that it has survived for so long. Even on High Pike, which is found to be an almost flat and grassy top, not at all like the impression it creates from below, a cairn is built on rocks overlooking Scandale, but the wall is higher still.

High Pike seen from Low Pike

21

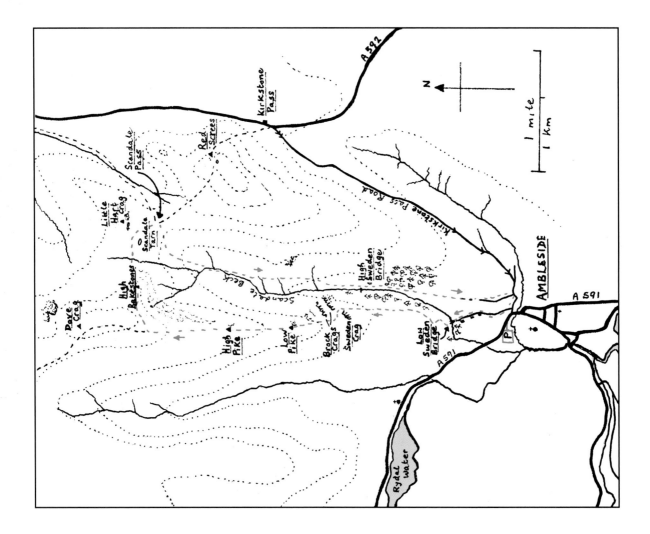

Rocks are now left behind as the path rises imperceptibly, on grass but with a few peaty sections, towards the broad grassy dome of Dove Crag. Ahead, but to the right, look for a fine tall cairn, possibly more than one, on High Bakestones. This is the next objective and just over half a mile from High Pike a pile of stones marks the point where a slender path curves to the right, eastwards. This has occasional cairns and initially contours across the slope but then descends slightly to reach a platform with outcropping slaty rocks overlooking steeper slopes towards Little Hart Crag and Scandale Pass. It is a grand viewpoint down Scandale and to the long slopes of Red Screes opposite. The main cairn is a fine, well-built stone man, about 8ft high and is easily identified. But it clearly presents a challenge to other, less expert, cairn-builders and I have several times found others in various stages of disintegration on this summit.

From here a path leads fairly steeply down the line of a shallow gill cutting through grass-covered tilted rocks slabs, then runs out onto easier grassy ground towards Little Hart Crag. Before reaching this, it crosses the infant Scandale Beck, curves just above the tiny Scandale Tarn and then follows the line of a collapsing wall down to a ladder-stile on the Scandale Pass.

Easy-angled slopes now trend downhill on a green path threading through patches of bracken to the valley floor at a gate and sheepfold. The path twice crosses the meandering Scandale Beck, then runs between stone walls set widely apart and over undu-

lating ground until it turns down sharply to the delightful stone arch of High Sweden Bridge which spans it. Continuing down the valley, between walls and through woodland and then with lovely views over to the parkland around Rydal, Sweden Bridge Lane leads to a junction with the Kirkstone Road.

A right turn here, steeply downhill towards the car park, will lead past the tempting Golden Rule pub. Need I say more?

The cairn, and some imposters, on High Bakestones

5.   Grasmere and Rydal

Best Map: OS 1:25,000 S.W. Sheet (Windermere and Kendal)

Distance: 5½ miles/8.8km

Highest elevation reached: 500ft/152m

Height gained: 250ft/76m

Overall star rating: * * *

General level of exertion required: Low

Time for the round: About 2½ hours

Terrain: Some road walking but mostly on good paths and all at low level so that it is ideal even for a day when the mists are well down the fellsides.

The round of Grasmere and Rydal Water (or just Rydal Water) must be the Lake District's most popular low-level walk. It is rightly so and has been held in great affection by generations of Lake District visitors. It has great literary associations of course with the Wordsworths, De Quincey and Coleridge which enhance its appeal. But even if those names mean nothing to you, this is a beautiful walk. And, perhaps surprisingly, it is possible to make some little variations to it which will give a different perspective even to those walkers who may know it already.

When starting from Grasmere, the best car park is that in Stock Lane as you enter the village from Ambleside (grid ref. 339073). Now walk back and cross the main road, take the lane past Dove Cottage and the Wordsworth Museum and up the hill, past an overgrown little pond on the left, swing left and then right, still uphill. As soon as the road levels off, do turn off it and go up onto White Moss Common – astonishingly few people do and it is only a hundred yards' diversion – for one of the loveliest views in the Lake District, that over Rydal Water. On returning to the road, keep on the level and as the now unmetalled way curves round the bend, you can see where it continues into the woods below Nab Scar. The bend is where a beck tumbles down a gill here and the normal walk continues along the same level as before. However, for a variation, climb the stile and take the footpath up the left bank of the gill towards what looks like a little dam. When you arrive, you find there's a tunnel through it but also a narrow path going to the right over its top, above the trees outside the intake wall but just below the shattered crags of Nab Scar where juniper, ash, holly and hawthorn have all seized hold. This pathway continues at a higher level and out of sight of the ordinary path until

Rydal Water from White Moss

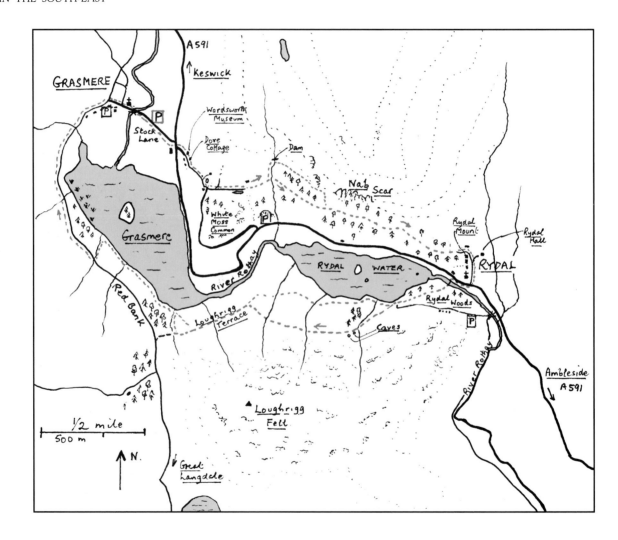

it rounds a corner and leads to a surprise on this steep hillside: a flat, grass sward about as big as a tennis-court – a marvellous place for a picnic.

Further progress at this level is blocked by a wall and steeper ground so you must descend and rejoin the main path, still delightful and now passing through woods and across sloping meadows, leading gently to the walled lane at Rydal, swinging downhill with the Mount on the right and the Hall on the left. Rydal Church is a little lower down and behind it the delightful Dora's Field, which – as well as an interesting brass plaque on a stone at its far end – also has some useful seats for contemplation of the sublime, or for just resting the legs.

Walk a few yards now to the main road, turn right and in another fifty take the footbridge over the Rothay, turn right and wander through the beautiful Rydal Woods. At the kissing-gate, you may continue beside the lake but it is more interesting to slant upwards a little to the wide gravel track which shortly climbs to pass the entrance to the lower of two great caves. Scrambling into this cave provides much fun for youngsters – and isn't as easy as it looks – but you can walk straight into the upper one.

Leaving the caves, follow the high-level path contouring the hillside below Loughrigg and well above Rydal Water, skirting above a wood of larch and birch to cross another shoulder for superb views of Grasmere. The path then leads round onto the level Loughrigg Terrace, from where more lovely landscape unfolds. Choose either a steep descent at the end of

Grasmere seen from Red Bank

the Terrace, or a slanting path before the end, towards the bridge over the Rothay at the outlet from Grasmere. Now take a path around the shore of the lake with views across the water to the little island and to the higher fells, all golden brown on their lower slopes and grey-green higher up. As the land becomes swampy, the path leads back to the Red Bank road. All that remains is the tarmac tramp down this road – the least interesting bit – but even now there are enchanting views over the wall and you soon reach the car again.

27

6. Butter Crag and Allcock Tarn

Best Map: OS 1:25,000 S.E. Sheet (Windermere
and Kendal)

Distance: 3 miles/4.8km

Highest elevation reached: 1150ft/351m

Height gained: 925ft/282m

Overall star rating: **/***

General level of exertion required: Medium

Time for the round: 2 hours

Terrain: Easy walking on good paths though the
descent may need care if wet, because wet
grass at a steep angle can be lethal.

Allcock Tarn lies to the east of Grasmere on a
rocky shelf, the northern end of which is Butter
Crag, about halfway up the flank of the main ridge
running from Nab Scar to Fairfield. It is a very
pleasant ascent and usually below the cloud ceiling
even on a wet day, giving views over the lovely vale of
Grasmere. No wonder William Wordsworth enjoyed
living here.

The most convenient starting-point is in Grasmere
village at the Stock Lane car park (grid ref. 339073).
Leaving this, turn left, walk back to the main A591
road and cross it to the secondary road signed for
Dove Cottage and the Wordsworth Museum. Walk
gently uphill a short way to a group of farm buildings,
a reedy pond on the left and a crossroads, then turn
left uphill (there's a sign 'Public footpath Allcock
Tarn' on the roadside). In a hundred paces, the track
leads off left again and quickly reaches a fork with a
National Trust sign 'Brackenfell'. The left-hand track
is closed by a gate in the wall, whereas the right-hand
one leads upwards outside it. In fact, the right-hand
way does lead, though more steeply and directly, via a
kissing-gate, between walls and up alternately rocky
and grassy paths, to Allcock Tarn, but it is not so
pleasant as the left-hand way.

So pass through the gateway and follow the track
which ascends through the trees, climbing in graceful
curves up the fellside and with the occasional seat
placed at a vantage-point. Pass a former circular
fishpond and then, as the track rises above the
woodland and becomes more of a path, skirt below
and then rise up to the little rocky height of Grey
Crag. This usually sports a flagpole as it is the highest
point of the Grasmere Sports senior fell-race held in
August each year. Some years ago, when I thought I

*Greenhead Gill and
Butter Crag seen
from Grasmere*

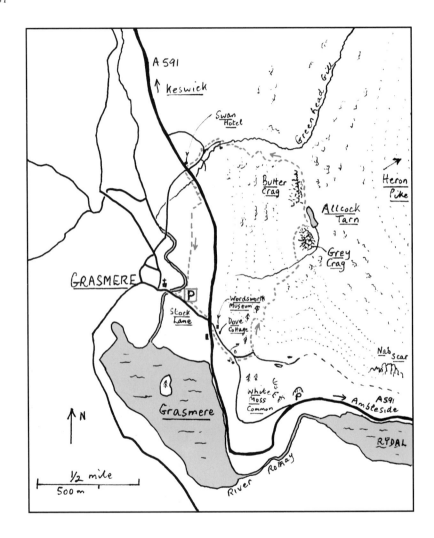

was fairly fit, I tried to see how far I could run up the course taken by the race. I did manage to actually run a little way beyond the first wall, slowed to a fast walk and then to a totter. I decided I wouldn't stand half a chance. I've been encouraged since, however, by noticing that during an actual race only a very few of the competitors can keep running further than that same wall.

Grey Crag is at the southern end of the shelf on which lies Allcock Tarn ('Alcock' on the OS map) so this is soon discovered by going on a little further and through the gateway in the wall. It can be a delightful sun-trap here; a most pleasant place to sit on the close-cropped grass and dangle your toes in the water.

To descend, follow the path leading alongside the tarn, over a stile at its northern end and then through a little rocky defile between Butter Crag on the left and the long uphill slope to Heron Pike on the right. Zigzags now lead downhill across the flank of Greenhead Gill and, keeping outside the wall, towards it. Once the shelter of the gill is reached, the trees shade the path which goes down it, a gate is reached, the path becomes a lane and, since there are now houses along the lane, it is metalled. Turn left at the junction and the main road is reached beside the Swan Hotel. Now go along the main road, but only for a hundred paces or so, before taking the (signed) public footpath on the right. This leads back via six gates or kissing-gates, easily and pleasantly across the meadows and so to Grasmere village again. The lads

(and lasses nowadays) who run the fell-race will all do the climb and be back in about twenty minutes – but they won't have had time to look at the view.

Storm clouds leaving Allcock Tarn

7. Wansfell Pike and Troutbeck

Best Map: OS 1:25,000 S.E. Sheet (Windermere and Kendal)

Distance: 6 miles/9.6km approx.

Highest elevation reached: 1581ft/482m

Height gained: 1400ft/427m

Overall star rating: */**

General level of exertion required: Fairly high on the way up, then easy

Time for the round: 3–3½ hours

Terrain: On good paths, but steep on the ascent. Most of the walk is at a low level and so enjoyable even in poor weather.

Wansfell Pike is actually the end of a long ridge running towards the Kirkstone Pass and it is easy to underestimate its ascent. But it does enable you to escape the crowds in Ambleside quickly, gives possibly the best view of the length of Windermere and, when combined with a return via Troutbeck, is a fine round.

The best car park is the main one on the left of the main road leaving Ambleside towards Keswick, just opposite the Charlotte Mason College (grid ref. 375046). Now head back towards the centre of the town to find the sign 'To the Waterfalls' which points between the Market Hall and Barclays Bank (itself next to the Salutation Hotel). A tarmac road now leads up the right bank of Stock Ghyll and after three hundred paces or so you should leave it to follow a track under the trees and very close to the rushing waters, for the beck comes down a series of cascades. There are plenty of seats and picnic spots and signs saying 'don't pick the flowers' or 'don't lean over the railings' and so on – for this a Beauty Spot and you'd better behave yourself.

Keep on the right bank towards a footbridge on the upper falls but bear right before reaching it and pass through the iron revolving gate which leads to a metalled road. A sign points the way up the road to Kirkstone Pass here and if you're ever inclined to walk up to Kirkstone on a quiet track, this is the way to go; if you try to walk up 'The Struggle', you'll be lucky to arrive alive. Walk up the road a little way and on the right there is a high ladder-stile and a sign to 'Troutbeck via Wansfell'. This is the way to go and the path climbs steadily but steeply, over more stiles and uphill through fields, with a final grind in low gear to the highest point. I must admit to a particular affection for the fine views now revealed, for I was just

The north-western slope up to Wansfell Pike from the Kirkstone Pass road

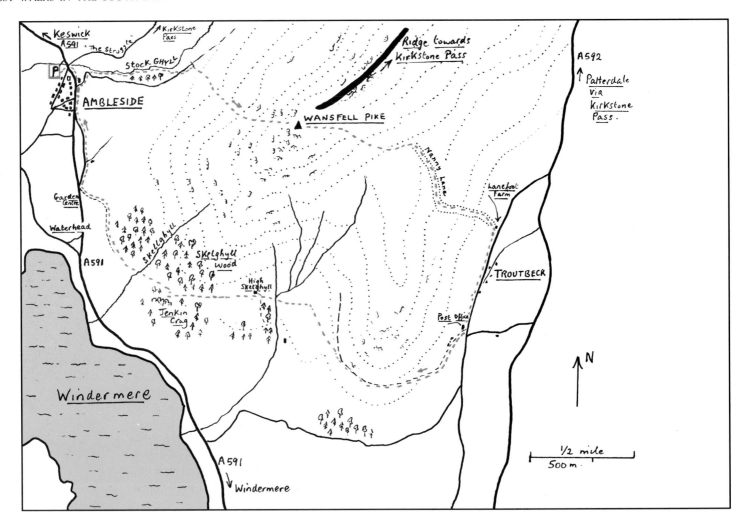

Keswick
A591

↖Kirkstone
Pass

"The Struggle"

Stock Ghyll

Ridge towards
Kirkstone Pass

WANSFELL PIKE

A592

↑Patterdale
via
Kirkstone
Pass.

AMBLESIDE

Nanny Lane

Lanefoot
Farm

Garden
Centre

Waterhead

A591

Skelghyll

Skelghyll
Wood

High
Skelghyll

TROUTBECK

Jenkin
Crag

Post Office

Windermere

↑N

A591

↓Windermere

½ mile

500 m

fifteen when, from here, I first saw the wonderful Lakeland fells laid out before me, to which I have returned countless times. On a recent visit, even though the weather was fairly foul and I was being pelted with rain, I watched a rainbow arching between Loughrigg Fell and Snarker Pike, with the spire of Ambleside Church in the middle: a lovely, if transient, sight.

There is a stile over the summit ridge wall and a sign to Troutbeck via Nanny Lane. Follow cairns gently down the moor to the east to reach this walled bridleway which leads down, alternately grassy and slaty, very pleasantly to emerge on the road between the buildings of Lanefoot Farm. Turn right here and follow the road for a little under half a mile until you spot the 'Bridleway Ambleside' sign just beyond the village post office. This walled track climbs steadily until Windermere and then Wansfell Pike come into view again as it curves round the hillside. Now leave the track for the footpath on the left, signed to 'Ambleside via Skelghyll and Jenkin Crag', which leads across fields towards High Skelghyll Farm. When the path meets the metalled track leading to the farm, turn up it. It becomes a bridleway again beyond the farm and soon enters Skelghyll Wood. Halfway through the wood is the little rocky outcrop of Jenkin Crag which seems, on wet or fine days alike, to attract a steady stream of visitors. I think it's another Beauty Spot. There are views over the head of Windermere from here, but they are fairly well obscured by the trees.

Leaving the crag, the path begins to descend through the woods, crossing Skelghyll itself by a bridge and offering several alternative ways down. Keep to the highest path now as it soon reaches a tarmac lane which quickly leads to the old road just above Hayes Garden Centre. Turn right and you are soon back in Ambleside.

The Kirkstone Pass from Wansfell Pike

8.   Silver How

Best Map: OS 1:25,000 S.E. Sheet (Windermere and Kendal)

Distance: 4 miles/6.4km approx.

Highest elevation reached: 1292ft/394m

Height gained: 1000ft/305m

Overall star rating: * *

General level of exertion required: Medium

Time for the round: 2½ hours

Terrain: A mixture of grassy, rocky and scree paths, almost all on the open fell.

Grasmere and Rydal Water are in the very heart of the National Park and Silver How is one of several minor fells whose ascent allows enchanting views over this delightful vale but is also a pleasure in itself.

Start in Grasmere village; the most convenient car park is that next to the new National Park Information Centre opposite St Oswald's Church (grid ref. 335074). There are many changes taking place in the centre of Grasmere but I hope it is safe to assume that the church will remain . . . From here, turn left, away from the village (on the road signed for Langdale and Coniston) which runs round the west side of the mere and then, avoiding the private drive across the meadow, go up the walled track opposite the boat-landings, clearly signed 'To Great Langdale'. This leads, via a kissing-gate, across a field with some fine larch and fir trees and also some splendid *roches moutonnées* (great rocks scoured smooth by moving ice and a reminder that it isn't so long ago that an Ice Cap covered the area) to another gate. Then pass up and across the hillside with the wall to your left which protects many fine trees from the depredations of the local sheep. The walls that keep out sheep don't keep out deer however and I have several times been for an early morning jog up the Red Bank road and seen them in the gardens of the houses along the way. When disturbed they leap and bound away into better cover and, from our experience, there are no such things as plants that deer will not eat.

There are good retrospective views from here across the vale, to Helm Crag, Seat Sandal and Fairfield and the fine gills that cut into their flanks. At the end of the rise the wall swings left and starts to descend and will lead eventually to Chapel Stile. Another path leads gently upwards across the fellside and, with a few kinks in it, will arrive at Harry Place Farm in

Silver How seen across Grasmere

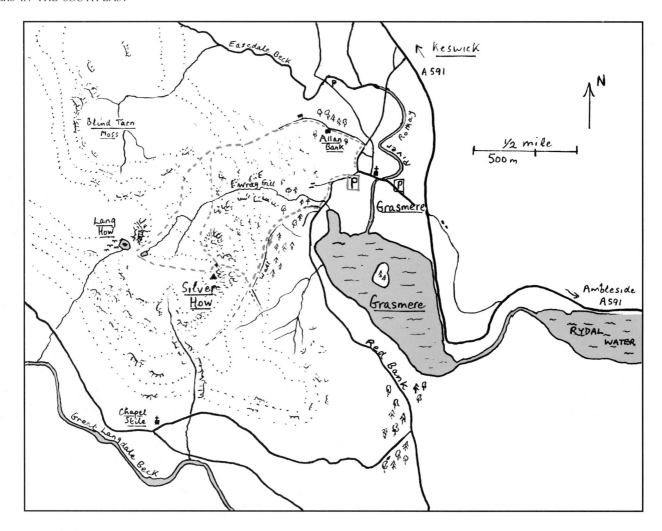

Langdale. Your way, however, should be still upwards, sharply right up the steep, grassy path which leads then up the little river of scree in a shallow gully. At the top, the view is over towards Easedale, and the summit of Silver How is just up to your left. The views are wide-ranging, particularly to the south-east; the shining waters of Grasmere, Rydal, Windermere, Coniston and Esthwaite Water can all be seen, as well as many lovely hills.

To descend, get onto the path heading down northwards towards Easedale. This skirts the edge of a depression or moss on Silver How's northern flank, in which rises Wray Beck, and just before the stream begins its plunge down the ravine of Wray Gill, the path crosses the stream into an area of juniper bushes.

If you fancy a further excursion before the descent, make your way along the fell-top towards the west (and the Langdale Pikes) where, about half a mile away, can be seen the rocky top of Lang How and, just out of sight below its crags, are two small tarns. The larger of these provides sanctuary during summer months for a screeching, squawking colony of black-headed gulls. If you get too close, however, you may well be warned away in a distinctly smelly manner. On leaving, follow the path north-west along the left-hand side of the moss, to reach the area of junipers at the top of Wray Gill.

The descent now continues steeply towards Easedale, over a stile, down a walled lane and so to a metalled one. This leads through open parkland beside Allan Bank, the beautifully situated house which was home to William Wordsworth and his family for three years, then easily to Grasmere village again.

Turn right on reaching the Red Lion Hotel, and the car park is a few paces away.

Grasmere and Rydal seen from Silver How

9.   Helm Crag and the Easedale Ridge

Best Map: OS 1:25,000 S.E. Sheet (Windermere
   and Kendal), overlapping with N.W. Sheet
   (Ennerdale and Derwent)

Distance: 5 miles/8km

Highest elevation reached: 1739ft/530m

Height gained: About 1450ft/442m

Overall star rating: */**

General level of exertion required: Medium

Time for the round: About 3 hours

Terrain: A steep ascent on a good path, then fair
   paths over peat and grass, which become stony
   on the last stages of the return.

The 'Lion and the Lamb' are distinctive rock features (not a pub!) on the summit of Helm Crag, the fell overlooking Grasmere village to the north, and provide an objective for a first-class walk. An alternative way to the one proposed could be to descend to Greenburn Bottom to the north, but that does involve a tramp back along the tarmac. The return along Far Easedale gives a more satisfying conclusion and the above should only be considered as an escape route in bad weather.

Either park in Grasmere, or preferably in the car park just up the Easedale road at grid ref. 334081 (there is no parking beyond here). Now continue to the little hamlet at the end of the metalled section; Helm Crag will be directly in view ahead. Signs lead up a walled lane to a level green pathway where a left turn leads up Far Easedale; however turn right instead to find an excellent path, created by the National Trust. This rises past an old quarry, continues steeply upwards on pitched stones to pass above Jackdaw Crag, then winds up grassier slopes to a shoulder. A last steep and rockier bit leads to the ridge crest and a jutting little crag overhanging the slopes above the Dunmail Raise road, which must surely be 'The Lion'? But a little further along the crest another crag does exactly the same thing. Both crags can look like the lion with the lamb at its feet, but it is the first that is best seen from Grasmere village.

The ridge stretches ahead but with a descent first to a saddle and then a climb up towards another rocky lump, Gibson Knott. You may descend from this saddle if you choose, for an infrequently-used grassy path leads down to the left towards a rock hump and then between walls, to link up with the path along the valley floor of Easedale, but it's a pity to abandon

Helm Crag seen from the descent from Allcock Tarn

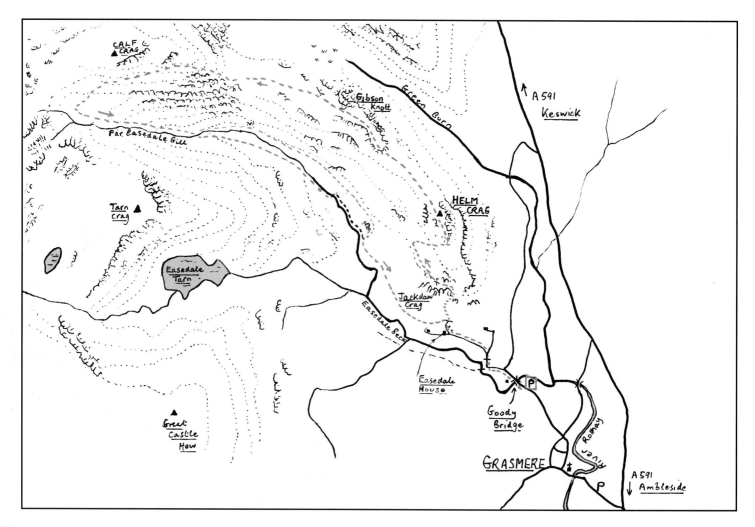

this fine ridge so soon. The ridge-path skirts to the left of the main line of Gibson Knott, but it is more sporting to follow the ridge itself which, although broad, has quite a lot of scramble-worthy slabs.

Ending this section, further than it looks from Helm Crag, is another descent to a broad saddle furnished with several cairns – noticeable since cairns are unusual on this ridge. Some walkers do descend here to the north into Greenburn Bottom, but will have to face the eventual walk along the tarmac that I mentioned earlier. The natural continuation however involves climbing gently upwards again up the blunt end of a steepening in the ridge towards its highest point (and that of the walk also) near Calf Crag. In fact, the path takes the easiest line and contours just south of the highest rocky bit, reaching a grassy hause at the head of Far Easedale. Here there is an iron ladder-stile set firmly in a non-existent fence: perhaps sleepless sheep count humans climbing it?

This is the point of return. An obvious path now leads south-east down Far Easedale although, when it crosses Far Easedale Gill to the south bank, it may be better to stay on the north bank and use a much drier sheep track leading down the valley until the intake walls are reached when a grassy slope enables the main path (now also on the north side) to be reached easily.

The final stretch goes along a most attractive part of the valley where rowans and holly bushes shade clear pools in the beck and there is many a tempting resting place in which to linger. Part of this last

section is between two walls of an ancient lane which, in winter, can turn into a watercourse; it is therefore incredibly stony and uneven underfoot for a while, but the path soon leads to the base of Jackdaw Crag where the outward route is rejoined. A right turn through the iron gate takes you back to the metalled road beside Easedale House and there just remains the stroll on the level road back to the car.

The 'Lion and Lamb' seen from the north side, looking towards Grasmere

10.   Whitbarrow Scar

Best Map: OS 1:50,000 1¼" to 1 mile (2cm to
    1km) Landranger Sheet 97 (Kendal &
    Morecambe). (Not on 1:25,000 scale maps)

Distance: 5–6 miles/8–9.6km

Highest elevation reached: 706ft/215m

Height gained: 680ft/207m

Overall star rating: *

General level of exertion required: Low/medium

Time for the round: 2–2½ hours

Terrain: Fair paths through woods and along
    limestone scarps.

It was always the great cliff of White Scar which
caught my eye when I turned off the A591 to go
west to Eskdale and Wasdale, for as the road crosses
the estuary at the end of the Lyth Valley, it is clearly
visible for about two miles and the road passes just
below its foot. Then there were days when I retreated
from the Lakes because the weather was awful, only to
find that it was clearing as I neared Kendal – and then
I wished I had somewhere to go for a walk before

going home. White Scar is in fact the southern end of
a fine limestone escarpment about seven miles south-
west of Kendal and it looked a likely place. So I
explored. Forgive me if, for a few moments, I tell you
about my mistakes so that you don't repeat them.

On my first visit, I went below the great white cliff
of White Scar, found a way up to the top by its
left-hand end and then traversed along above the cliff
into the woods seeking a way down to the north-east.
Within two hundred feet of the car, I was almost
vertically above it and in thick forest and I had to
retrace my steps entirely.

Then I looked more carefully and worked out a
complete round that would start in the north-east at
the little hamlet of Row just beyond the Lyth Valley
Hotel, climb to the ridge, walk its length north to
south, descend White Scar and return along the
valley bottom using the paths and tracks clearly
marked on the map. This is perfectly feasible, so long
as you can arrange to be collected on your descent.
You'll have to climb a wall or two getting up to the
ridge, then you can walk its length successfully. But I
didn't have a driver and it is a complete disaster trying
to use the paths to get back to Row village, for even
when you find them, they're completely overgrown or
barred by barbed-wire. What should have taken an
hour at the most took me nearly two and a half, and

White Scar

45

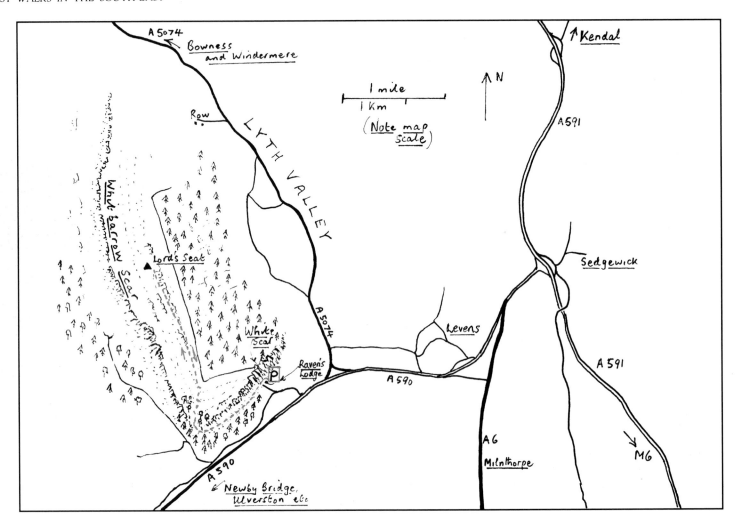

A 5074

Bowness
and Windermere

↑ Kendal

Row

LYTH VALLEY

1 mile

1 Km

(Note map scale)

↑ N

A 591

White barrow Scar

▲ Lord's Seat

A 5074

Sedgewick

White Scar

Levens

A 591

P Raven's Lodge

A 590

A 6

A G
Milnthorpe

↓ MG

A 590

← Newby Bridge,
Ulverston etc

some ripped clothing. So, instead of a round, this time you'll have to go up and down the same way. But it really is worth it.

From the A6 or the A591, turn onto the A590 for Newby Bridge, Ulverston and the towns of west Cumbria. Just past the A5074 junction to Windermere, take the slip-road across the carriageway directly towards White Scar. Follow the signs for 'Raven's Lodge' and park just beyond the farm buildings (grid ref. 461852). A track climbs to the left below the huge cliff and runs out onto a great limestone pavement which I believe is called a 'bedding-plane' by geologists. It is surprisingly smooth and is exposed for about a quarter of a mile at the foot of the crags before it comes to an end. It was obviously used as a roadway for the former quarry operations. There is clearly no way of climbing to get above the scar until you have turned the corner, but the crags are becoming less steep as you approach it and they decline into a wooded shoulder, up which a pathway sneaks. You have little idea where you are for a while, but just stay on the path and you emerge onto the open heath above the woodland. Take notice of your position because you'll need to find it on the return. Now it's all space and open air; fine walking along the limestone edges. The awful massed conifers are fenced off just below the high land on the eastern side but on the heath there are only twisted junipers here and there and, in the area around Lord's Seat (the highest point) – where there is a large and solid cairn with a plaque commemorating Canon Hervey, Founder of

On Whitbarrow Scar, near Lord's Seat

the Lake District Naturalists Trust – there are an enormous number of anthills, so be careful where you sit down.

As you retrace your steps, go just a little further to the edge of the White Scar cliffs and views over the estuary towards Morecambe Bay are revealed. All you have to do now is to remember how to get down.

INDEX

Page numbers in **bold** refer to walks; those in *italics* to illustrations.

Allcock Tarn **29–31**, *31*
Ambleside 21, 33, 35

Black Fell *12*, **13–15**
Butter Crag 28, **29–31**

Calf Crag 43
Colwith **9–11**

Dove Crag 21

Elterwater 8, **9–11**

Far Easedale 41, 43
Far Easedale Gill 43

Gibson Knott 41, 43
Glen Mary Bridge 13
Grasmere (lake) 36, 39
Grasmere (village) *19*, **25–7**, *27*, 29, 31, 37, 39, 41
Great Langdale Beck 9
Greenburn Bottom 41, 43
Greenhead Gill 28, 31
Grey Crag 29, 31

Helm Crag *2*, *40*, **41–3**, *43*
High Bakestones 21, 23, *23*
High Brock Crag 21
High Pike *20*, **21–3**
High Sweden Bridge 23
Horn Crag 41

Jackdaw Crag 41, 43

Iron Keld Plantation 15

Kirkstone Pass 33, 35

'Lion and the Lamb' *2*, 41, 43
Langdale Pikes 8
Lingmoor Fell 11
Little Hart Crag 21, 23
Little Langdale **9–11**
Little Langdale Tarn 11
Lord's Seat 47
Loughrigg Fell *16*, **17–19**
Loughrigg Terrace 19, 27
Low Arnside 15
Low Brock Crag 21
Low Pike *20*, 21
Low Sweden Bridge 21

Nab Scar 25
Nook Lane 21

Red Bank 17, 27
Rothay, River 17, 27
Rydal 17, 19, 27
Rydal Water 17, *24*, **25–7**

Scandale **21–3**
Scandale Beck 21, 23
Scandale Tarn 23
Scandale Pass 23
Silver How 36, **37–9**
Slater Bridge *11*, 11
Sweden Bridge Lane 23
Sweden Crag 21

Tom Heights *12*, **13–15**
Tarn Hows 13
The Tarns 13
Tongue Intake Plantation 15
Troutbeck **33–5**

Wansfell Pike *32*, **33–5**
Whitbarrow Scar **45–7**
White Scar 44, 45

Yew Tree Tarn 13, 15